Editor Verity Weston
Editorial Assistant June Dale
Design Roland Blunk MSIA
Picture Research Brigitte Arora
Production Rosemary Bishop

First published 1979
Reprinted 1981, 1983

Macdonald & Co. (Publishers) Ltd
Maxwell House
Worship Street
London EC2A 2EN

ISBN 0 356 05951 0

Made and printed by
Waterlow Ltd., Dunstable
England

Artists
Terry Allen Designs Ltd: 6–7
Roland Blunk: 12(T)
Dick Eastland: 16–17, 18–19
Richard Hook/Temple Art: 4–5,
20–21, 24–25
Peter North: 32–33, 44–45
Tony Payne: 12(B), 13, 14–15, 23,
27, 29(R), 31(T), 39(BR)
George Thompson: 9

Contents

Seasons of the Eskimo

"And yet there is only one great thing,
the only thing, to live,
to see in tents and on journeys the great day that dawns
and the light that fills the world."

In the cold and desolate lands which surround the North Pole, a unique group of people have made their home: the Eskimos.

The Eskimos did not know that anyone else existed, so they called themselves *Inuit*—the People. They had their own way of life, which helped them not just to survive in their bleak Arctic land, but to enjoy it, and make the most of living there.

The Eskimos perfected special ways of hunting the animals which supplied them with food, clothing, and raw materials for many other uses. They also developed forms of clothing and shelter which were exactly right for the harsh Arctic environment.

The seasons

Even with their special skills life was never easy. The Eskimos depended completely for all their needs on success at hunting. This meant that their whole way of life was adjusted to fit in with the seasons, for these brought in their wake the different animals the Eskimos needed so much.

The seasonal movements of the Eskimos in search of caribou, seals or walrus, were a closely interwoven part of their life. The Eskimos' joy at travelling, seeing new places and meeting new people is expressed in the old Eskimo song, above.

The pattern of life

To the Eskimo, it was not a troublesome break from routine to move camp from the sea ice to the land, or from igloo to tent at the end of spring: it was the very pattern of life itself. Eskimos were bound to seasonal movements just as firmly as animals were. They had a deep understanding of the balance of Arctic nature of which they were just one part.

Left Here a group of Eskimos are preparing to leave their camp to hunt walrus. They will have to face many dangers, and the hunters are excited at the prospect of their long journey.

The Eskimo in the foreground is lashing on to his sledge the equipment his wife is bringing. Only he must do this, for his life may depend on knowing exactly where this equipment is in an emergency.

Inuit Nunangat

"The land is so beautiful with its high rivers and lakes waiting to be fished. It has great mountains, and images form as if there could be caribou among them. Caribou sometimes come peeping round the hills."
Rosie Paulla from Gjoa Haven, Canada

Right Groups of Eskimos who settled in different areas of the Arctic developed very different ways of life to suit the natural conditions they found. The inland Caribou Eskimos obtained almost everything they needed from the great herds of caribou, whereas the East Greenland Eskimos satisfied their needs from seals and bears.

Below The early Eskimos came from Asia and many years ago they occupied a much larger area of the Arctic than they do now.

The first Eskimos were descendants of groups of hunters who reached the North American continent from Asia between 10 and 15 thousand years ago. Sea levels were lower then and the continents were linked by land.

Some of the groups moved eastwards along the Arctic coasts and plains.

A way of life

As these early Eskimos spread slowly eastwards looking for new hunting grounds, they began to develop the skills which were to be the key to living in their new homeland. But it was not until about 4000 years ago that the Dorset Culture appeared.

The Dorset Eskimos were successful hunters although their weapons were simple. They had invented sledges, but had no dogs. They had *kayaks* but had not learned how to hunt from them. For 3000 years the Dorset Eskimos extended over the whole Arctic region, until 1000 years ago a dramatic change took place: the Thule Culture (pronounced *Too'lay*) appeared.

The Thule Culture

The people called the Thule Eskimos came from the Amundsen Gulf region of Canada and were much more skilled than the Dorset Eskimos. They had dogs to pull their sledges and from their skin boats they hunted whale and walrus.

Within 400 years Thule Eskimos spread across the Arctic from Alaska to East Greenland. They spoke basically the same language over a vast area, 6500km across the Arctic. They had become the true *Inuit*, the People, ancestors of all modern Eskimos, and they had truly made the Arctic *Inuit Nunangat*, the People's Land.

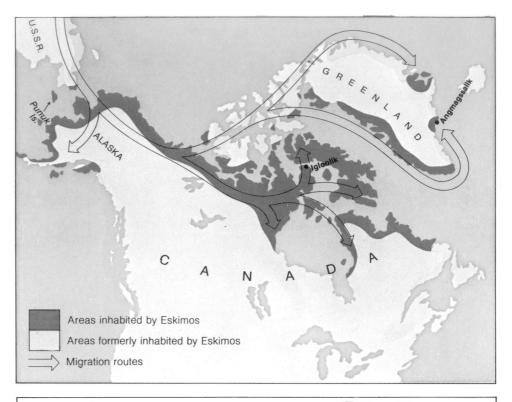

Areas inhabited by Eskimos

Areas formerly inhabited by Eskimos

Migration routes

We know how and where the Eskimos lived thousands of years ago from the things archaeologists find in their old houses and graves.

Each different culture, or way of life, left behind different objects which help us to understand how the Eskimos of old lived.

Above Dorset Culture. Polar bear carved in walrus ivory. 16cm long. Igloolik area.

Above Okvik Culture (about the same period as Thule). Head carved in walrus ivory, 8cm high. Punuk Islands.

Above Thule Culture. Figure carved in wood, 8cm high. Angmagssalik, E. Greenland.

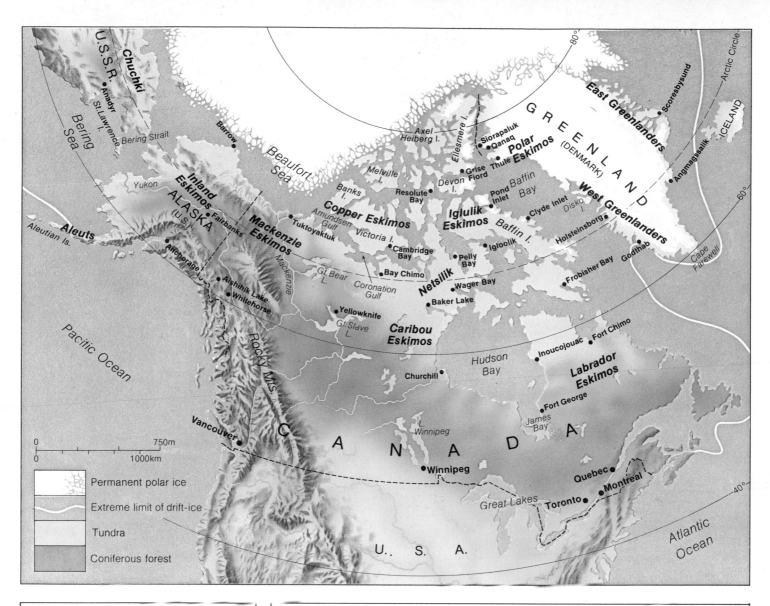

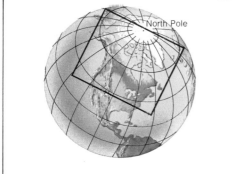

Above As the earth rotates around the sun, the axis it turns around is tilted at 23½° from the vertical.

Right Because of the 23½° tilt the Arctic receives very little sunlight during the winter. This is why there is a long period of winter darkness and it is so cold. In summer there is sunlight for 24 hours a day. Then the Arctic regions are pointing to the sun for the whole 24 hours which the earth takes to make one rotation.

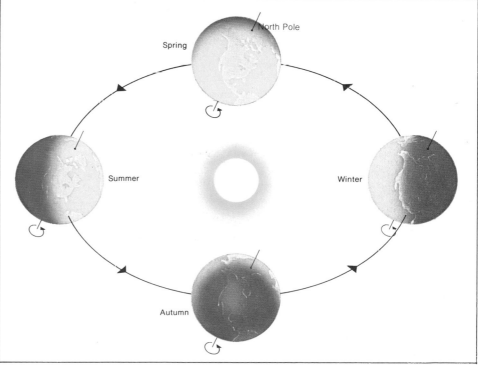

Imak: the sea

The ice which fills the Arctic Basin is always revolving slowly round the North Pole. Some is pushed south through the narrow gaps between the land masses, and drifts south until it finally melts. The ice is usually about three metres thick and is rough and jagged because of pressure from winds and currents.

In winter and spring, when the ice movement is least, the Eskimos roam the ice. It is their highway and larder, and across its cold vastness they seek their battles with *Nanok*, the polar bear.

Plankton

By late spring the sea ice is beginning to break up. The air rings with the creaks and groans of the melting, collapsing ice. This is the time the Eskimos avoid the ice and the only time they are not masters of it.

Below the shifting ice is a different world. Tiny single-cell creatures called plankton are multiplying in response to the increased sunlight. The walrus and seals which live in the Arctic waters all year are joined by migrating whales, seals and thousands of sea birds. They are all returning with the sun to benefit from the plankton.

For thousands of years the coastal Eskimos made their homes close to waters where they could hunt all this marine life. For them the sea provided everything.

Adrift on the ice

In 1872 the ship *Polaris* was sunk in Baffin Bay. Two Eskimo families were among 19 of the crew marooned on the ice. For 197 days they drifted before being rescued off Labrador.

During the long drift the Eskimo men kept the party alive by catching the plentiful sea birds and animals.

Fishes of the Arctic seas. The Arctic char and the capelin are most important to the Eskimos. Angmagssalik in East Greenland is named after the Eskimo word for capelin.

Capelin

Polar cod

Arctic char

Halibut

Above Harbour seals are one of the most common types found in the Arctic.

Left Walrus are sociable animals and like to gather together when not searching for food.

Below *Nanok,* the polar bear, or the "Great Wanderer", may travel hundreds of kilometres over ice in search of food. On land, sea and ice *Nanok* has no enemies other than man. The Eskimos believe that animals have souls the same as people and call the polar bear "the one who is closest to us".

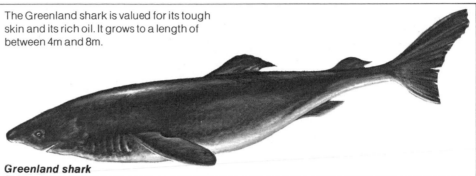

The Greenland shark is valued for its tough skin and its rich oil. It grows to a length of between 4m and 8m.

Greenland shark

The Arctic seas provide food for many sea birds in summer. In winter they all migrate to warmer parts of the world. The Arctic tern flies more than 20,000 km to spend the northern winter in the Antarctic.

Tern

Sabine's gull

Fulmar

Ross's gull

King eider

Little auk

Guillemot

Nuna: the land

North of the treeline, mile after mile of rolling rocky landscape known as tundra stretches northwards to the shores of the Arctic Ocean.

In winter the tundra is a harsh land, dark, cold and covered by a blanket of snow blown into strange shapes by the wind. But in summer it can be a pleasant place, its life awakened by the returning sun.

Thousands of birds fly north to breed in its vast spaces. The Arctic char swim up the rivers to spawn. Millions of colourful flowers bloom in the short summer. For animals and people this is a good time.

Left The Arctic hare is common throughout the tundra region and also the high Arctic lands of the extreme north. The Eskimos use its fur for making the soft socks which fit inside their *kamiks,* or outer boots.

Reindeer moss and caribou

The tundra vegetation provided the Eskimos with many edible plants and berries, but it was important to them for another reason: the tundra was rich in reindeer moss (not really a moss, but a lichen) so the caribou were able to live there. And to the Copper and Caribou Eskimos, the caribou was life itself.

The cycle of life

The Arctic animals fitted into a pattern of life and death. The death of a musk ox or caribou meant life for a family of wolves: the death of a wolf provided pickings for Arctic foxes, snowy owls and ravens.

The death of any of these gave food to many other small mammals, insects and birds which shared the Arctic world, for example, lemmings and voles. When these died their bodies added richness to the soil, and helped plants to grow, making food for more musk ox and caribou.

The Arctic animals were important to the Eskimo. To benefit from them, he fitted into the Arctic life cycle, without disturbing the pattern which nature had already established.

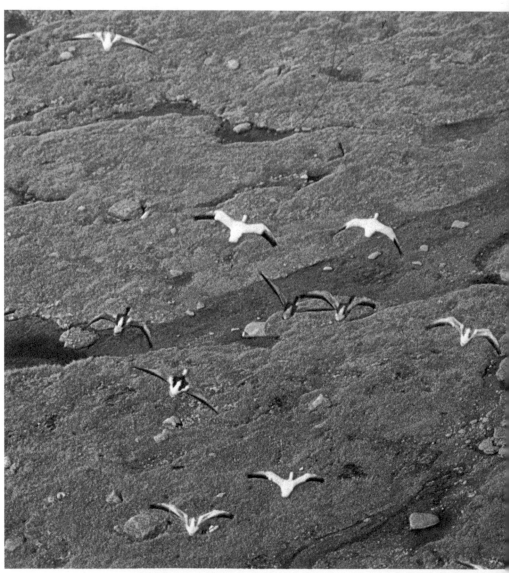

Above Each year the herds of caribou come north to graze on the tundra in summer. In winter they return to the shelter of the sub-arctic forests. The Eskimos rely on this regular pattern of movement in planning their autumn caribou hunts.

Left The musk ox lives all year round in the lonely islands and mountain ranges north of the tundra. The Eskimos call these lands *Uming-maknuna*, Musk Ox Land. The only enemies of the musk ox are the polar wolves which live in the remotest areas of the Arctic.

Above Arctic foxes are found everywhere in the Arctic: this one carries a dead hare. Their silver coloured winter skins make women's trousers and jackets.

Left At first sight the tundra appears to be a barren land. In fact it supports a rich and varied animal and plant life. Every year thousands of birds such as these geese come to breed here.

Keeping warm

"In this well ventilated costume the man will sleep upon his sledge with the atmosphere 93 degrees below our freezing point."
Elisha Kent Kane, the American explorer, writing in 1853 about Eskimo clothing

Below When a strong wind blows across the ice the Eskimo needs much warmer clothing. The table shows that a wind of only 20mph (32kph) makes a normal winter temperature of –30°C feel like –54°C. Even a mild day with a temperature of –5°C and little wind, will feel like –17°C when a wind of only 15mph (24kph) is blowing. The blue zone indicates great danger of exposed flesh being frozen: the red area indicates some danger, and the yellow zone is almost comfortable.

To the Eskimos, clothing was more important than fire and just as important as food for survival. To exist in the Arctic they adopted the methods of creatures already living there: the bear, the caribou, the fox, the hare, the wolf, the seals and birds. They used the skins of all of them to make clothes. The skins were sewn together with narwhal or caribou sinew, using needles of bone or ivory.

Air the insulator
The animal's fur kept it warm because of the air trapped within it. When the Eskimos took the fur they had the use of this warmth. But they also had the advantage of being able to have several layers of fur of different thicknesses and properties. So they had a set of clothes which trapped air within each layer and between layers also.

When an Eskimo stood still the warm air was trapped close to his body. When he ran, the clothes flapped and made the air circulate and cool him. This way sweating was reduced. Sweat-moistened clothes were dangerous, for damp furs quickly lost their insulating properties and froze solid if they cooled again.

Caribou hair
From end to end of the Arctic the Eskimo's clothing was more or less the same. Caribou was by far the most commonly used skin for clothing. It was extremely warm and light. A complete winter outfit weighed only about five kilograms.

It did have one big disadvantage: the hairs were hollow and broke off easily. They got into everything! Eskimos said you were not a man until you had eaten your own weight in caribou hairs.

	Wind speed MPH							
Temperature °C	5	10	15	20	25	30	35	40
5	2	–1	–4	–7	–9	–12	–12	–12
0	–4	–9	–12	–15	–18	–18	–20	–21
–5	–7	–12	–17	–18	–21	–23	–24	–26
–10	–12	–18	–23	–26	–29	–32	–34	–35
–15	–18	–26	–32	–34	–37	–40	–42	–43
–20	–23	–31	–40	–42	–45	–48	–50	–51
–25	–29	–40	–45	–51	–54	–57	–59	–60
–30	–32	–43	–51	–54	–59	–62	–64	–65
–35	–37	–51	–57	–62	–68	–70	–73	–74
–40	–43	–57	–65	–70	–76	–79	–81	–82
–45	–48	–62	–73	–78	–84	–87	–90	–91
–50	–57	–70	–79	–84	–93	–95	–98	–101

Preparing skins for clothing is a job which is always done by the women.
Left The blubber and fat are first scraped from the skin.

Below left The skin is stretched, either on a frame or by pegging it out on the ground, until it is absolutely dry.

Below The dry, stiff skin is softened by chewing. It can then be cut into the necessary shapes for clothing or *kamiks*.

Inner clothing

Outer clothing

Inner clothing

Outer clothing

Above The Polar Eskimo's clothing made use of the skins of a number of animals.

Both men and women wore hooded shirts made of bird skins. It took about 100 little auk skins to make one shirt which was worn with the feathers inside. On their legs the men wore trousers made of polar bear fur. This was very warm, and dirt fell off easily.

The women wore short fox skin pants but had longer *kamiks*, or boots, than the men. The women's *kamiks* were made of seal skin with fur removed. They had a stiff piece of skin inside and came well above the knee.

The men's *kamiks* were made of the same material but were much shorter. Hare skin socks were worn inside their *kamiks* by both men and women. Hare skin was used for socks as it always remained soft and warm.

In very cold conditions the Eskimos used outer *kamiks* made of caribou leg skins. Both men and women carried fox tails to put round their legs where *kamiks* and trousers met.

On top of the bird skin shirts the Eskimos wore a caribou skin *kooletah*. These were cut so that the animal's head formed the hood. The caribou's ears were left on to act as

ventilation holes. In summer the women had a lighter sealskin coat with a large hood or *amaut* in which a child could be carried.

Gloves were made of sealskin, and for use in *kayaks* sometimes had two thumbs, so the palm and back could be reversed when one got wet.

13

Journeys

Knud Rasmussen, who was half Eskimo, once said, "*Give me winter, give me dogs, and you can keep the rest.*"

All Eskimos shared in the joy of sledge travel. They were excited at the prospect of seeing new places and liked travelling for its own sake.

Using simple natural materials, the Eskimos invented the sledge and the *kayak* which made such journeys possible. They were able to live off the land while travelling and needed to carry only a few weapons and pieces of equipment. Thus they were able to travel great distances on their hunting expeditions.

In partnership with their dogs, which they valued more than anything else, the Eskimos were masters of land, sea and ice.

Sledges

There were many different types of sledge, all designed to be built and repaired easily, and to be flexible. A heavily loaded sledge had to be flexible to resist the battering it received when crossing rough ice. So the Eskimos lashed the various parts of the sledge together with leather thongs.

Kayaks and *umiaks*

The *kayak* was one of the most graceful craft ever invented. It enabled the Eskimos to glide softly through the water and come within harpooning distance of seals and walrus. The *kayak* was really a hunting craft and for long distance travelling the *umiak* would be used.

Both *kayaks* and *umiaks* were very light. They could easily be carried by hand or sledge over land or ice. But due to the extensive snow and ice of the Arctic the Eskimos made most of their long journeys by sledge.

Left The *umiak* was normally up to 9m long, and made of seal skins stretched over a framework of wood or bone. In Greenland it was used as a cargo boat and usually managed by the women. In Alaska however the Eskimos used their *umiaks* with a crew of eight or nine men to hunt the giant bowhead whales.

Right Because the *kayak* was smaller than the *umiak* it was very unstable. As most Eskimos could not swim they learned to use the paddle to "roll" the *kayak* upright if it capsized while they were in it.

The Copper Eskimos used their dogs to carry packs when they moved camp in summer.

The Alaskan Eskimo's sledge was narrow and designed to be pulled along forest trails by dogs tied in pairs to a central trace.

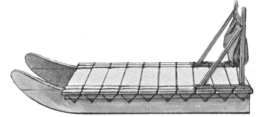

The sledges of the Polar Eskimos were broad and solid. They had narrow runners for travelling over the hard blue sea ice. Such a sledge was pulled by up to 14 dogs in a "fan" formation.

In East Greenland there was a lot of soft snow each winter. The sledges had broad runners and were lightly built to prevent them sinking in too much.

Survival

*"Difficult times, shortages of meat
have smitten everyone :
stomachs hollow, meat racks empty.
Aj-ja-japape."*
**A song recalling times of famine, by Tutlik, an
Iglulik Eskimo woman**

All the Eskimos' skills at hunting and travelling were aimed at finding food. All their great journeys were part of their never-ending search for meat.

The Arctic lands and seas contained an abundance of different foods and the Eskimos developed the skills necessary to harvest these riches. They were not particular about what they ate. If it was alive and they could catch it, they would eat it, all of it!

Diet

Eskimos ate and enjoyed every part of the creatures they killed. They had to, to obtain the vitamins otherwise missing from an all-meat diet.

Birds, for instance, were eaten whole. Only a few feathers and the beak were left to show that a hungry Eskimo had passed.

Sometimes meat was boiled, but the Eskimos had no objection to raw or even frozen meat, and often preferred it that way.

Many of the creatures which the Eskimos caught were only available at certain seasons. So the Eskimos had to store them, and produced some unusual foods. *Mattak*, for instance, was the skin of the narwhal. Kept outside for many months with the blubber attached, it was considered a delicacy. When eaten it was very chewy, with a nutty flavour.

Feast and famine

Although there was often plenty of food, there were also hard times. Eskimos always shared the results of their hunting amongst everyone in their camp. This helped them get through times of scarcity. But when disaster struck and food supplies dried up, it was not unusual in the old days for Eskimos to die of starvation.

Right On the tundra the Eskimos found a number of berries which were good to eat. The most common were the bilberry, crowberry and cranberry.

Below The Eskimos used every part of the seal. As well as food it supplied them with skins for clothing and harpoon lines, and blubber and oil for the lamps.

The first piece to be used was the liver. When the seal was caught it was cut out and eaten raw by the hunters who were present.

Bilberry

Crowberry

Cranberry

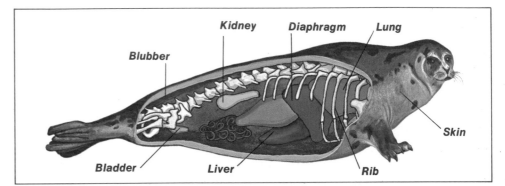

Blubber · Kidney · Diaphragm · Lung · Skin · Bladder · Liver · Rib

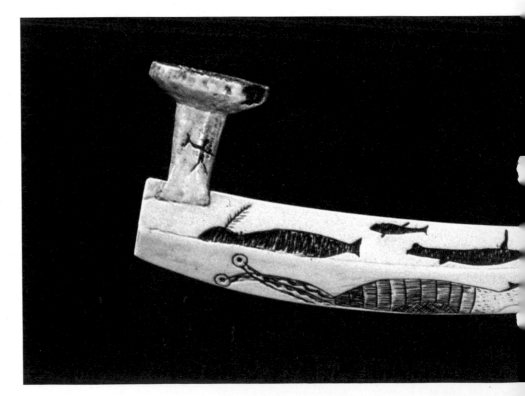

Right Ice fishing or "jigging" was practised by some groups of Eskimos. The fish were laid out round the hole so that their spirits could return to the water.

Below While they were inland hunting caribou, the Eskimos often visited traditional fishing places. The fish were guided by rows of rocks towards the waiting Eskimos who caught them on special spears called leisters.

Little auks returning to their nests in the cliffs were caught in nets.

The birds were collected together and prepared for storage.

About 800-1000 birds were packed into a complete sealskin.

The full skin was stored under rocks away from sunlight for six months.

Above *Kiviak* was a delicacy, often eaten at parties. The little auks, soaked through with seal's blubber, were eaten whole. The skins and feathers were pulled off. Stomach and intestines tasted bitter, like beer, and the flesh was spicy.

Left An ivory pipe with scrimshaw decoration of whaling scenes, done by filling scratches with soot. Eskimos learned scrimshaw from European whalers. (The Eskimos hunted the whale, and used every part of it, as they did with the seal.)

Puise : the seal

"... the tension made my body longer,
I drove my harpoon down
and tied him to the harpoon line."
**Igpakuhak of the Copper Eskimos, Victoria
Island, Canada**

Far out on the sea ice a cloud of
condensation hangs in the still air. It
is the frozen breath of a fur-clad
Eskimo standing motionless over an
aglu, a seal breathing hole, his
harpoon ready in his hand.

Suddenly the feather, which he has
carefully placed over the hole,
flutters, showing that a seal is
breathing below. The Eskimo
plunges his harpoon downwards with
tremendous force and the sea water in
the hole turns red with blood.
Another ringed seal has fallen victim
to the patience of an Eskimo hunter.

This method of hunting is known
as the *maupok*, or waiting method,
and is used in winter and early spring.

Utok

In late spring and summer seals lie
on the ice close to their breathing
holes. To hunt them Eskimos use
the *utok* or crawling method.

The Eskimo crawls towards the
seal as it takes a short nap, and pauses
when it wakes up. The seal is rather
short-sighted and thinks the Eskimo
is another seal.

When the hunter is close enough
he waits for the seal to doze off again
before throwing his harpoon.
Immediately he must run and catch
hold of the seal which, even though
dying, may otherwise slither into its
hole and be lost.

The Giver of Life

Without the seal the Arctic would be
a land without people. The great
numbers of seals along the Arctic
coasts kept the early Eskimos alive on
their long migrations. Since then the
Eskimos have continued to rely on
the seals, not only for food but also
for skins and blubber. It was so
important that the Eskimos gave it
the title "Giver of Life".

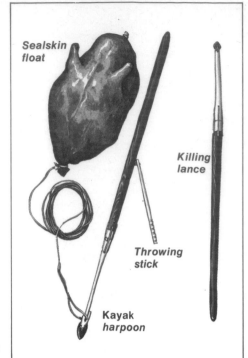

Right The Eskimos invented special weapons
for hunting seals from their *kayaks*.

With the throwing stick the Eskimos could
throw their harpoons with deadly accuracy up
to 45m. Once the harpoon had struck, the head
came off the shaft. The head was attached by
line to the *avatak* or seal skin bladder. The
hunter threw the *avatak* overboard to slow the
seal down. He could then kill it with his lance.

Sealskin float

Killing lance

Throwing stick

Kayak harpoon

Below The Polar Eskimo hunter Jakob Petersen
out in his *kayak* near Qanaq, North Greenland.

Left In 1824 Captain Lyon accompanied Captain Parry on his voyage to search for a north-west passage to India. Lyon's drawings were some of the first accurate records of Eskimo life to reach Europe. Here an Eskimo is hunting a seal by the *utok* method.

Below The *maupok* or waiting method requires great patience. The hunter may have to stand over the hole for many hours in temperatures around −30°C.

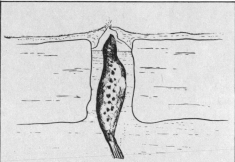

The seal keeps its breathing holes open as the ice thickens in winter.

The Eskimo places a feather in the narrow part of the hole.

Then he must wait, absolutely still, with harpoon ready.

The seal breathes, the feather moves and the Eskimo must strike.

Hunting the caribou

*"It's wonderful to hunt caribou,
but all too seldom one succeeds
standing like a bright fire over the plain."*
Piuvkak, from the Great Fish River of Canada

The great stream of fat healthy caribou, (which one Eskimo songwriter likened to a plague of maggots!) meant that a plentiful supply of meat and skins was at hand. This was important as the long dark winter months were not far away.

Long before the caribou were expected several Eskimo families assembled at camps near one of the routes the caribou always used.

Inugsuks

The men and boys scrambled up on the low rocky ridges above the camp to check that the previous winter's storms had not damaged the *inugsuks*. These were stone cairns in the rough form of human figures, which had been built by the Eskimos many years before.

The approaching caribou saw the *inugsuks* and thought they were men or wolves. They turned away and therefore passed the place where the hunters were lying in ambush.

The killing

As the leaders of the herd of caribou advanced the hunters picked up their bows and arrows. It was a long tense wait until the main part of the slow-moving herd was close enough for them to open fire. If they were lucky the stricken caribou fell to the ground without frightening the rest of the herd. Then the hunters quickly fired again, with a deadly accuracy gained from years of experience.

The Eskimos used simple weapons, so even on a good hunt the number of caribou they were able to kill was small, compared with the many thousands in the herd. In this way the Eskimo and the caribou existed together: the Eskimo needed the caribou, but he hunted them so that their survival was not threatened.

Hunting camps were often close to lakes and rivers which caribou had to cross. Copper Eskimos attacked the caribou on the land, and harpooned the swimming beasts from their *kayaks*. After a successful hunt the beaches would be strewn with dead bodies waiting to be cut up by the women.

Shelter

Below The Polar Eskimo Sekugssuk building his igloo during a bear hunting expedition. The party of Eskimos decided to camp because they noticed bad weather approaching. Sekugssuk's companions put up ordinary tents. In the storm which came that night their tents blew down and they too had to build igloos.

When the first Eskimo families reached the Arctic they had to make some sort of shelter for themselves. In summer each family lived in an easily moved skin tent, made of a double layer of seal or caribou skin supported on a framework of wood or bone. It gave good protection.

The winter house

When winter came the Eskimos usually built low rock houses with floors sunk into the ground. These houses were roofed with large slabs of rock, and turf was piled against the walls to keep the heat in.

For many years this type of house was used. At first the houses were small and square. Later they became larger and more rounded in shape, with long entrance passages and raised sleeping platforms at the rear.

With the seal-oil lamps burning, it was very cosy in such a house. But even in winter the Eskimos had to hunt to survive. It was this need to travel in winter which produced the igloo.

Igloo

Igdlu is the Eskimo word for any sort of house. In its English form, "igloo", it has come to mean just the snow houses which the Eskimos built for temporary shelter while travelling.

The Eskimos used blocks of wind-hardened snow to make their igloos. They were circular in plan and the snow blocks were laid in a rising spiral to form a dome. The last block was fitted by an Eskimo working from the inside. He then cut his way out and formed the entrance.

When an Eskimo hunter lay back on the sleeping platform he was very comfortable. The snow walls of his igloo kept him safe from the fiercest of Arctic storms.

Below in summer Eskimos used skin tents.
1 First the sleeping platform rocks were set out and the three main poles put up.

2 Rocks or wood were used to form the platform.

3 The rest of the poles and the small platforms for the lamps were added.

4 The skin tent was put over the poles and weighted down with rocks.
In severe weather an outer tent was also used.

Below Igloos were used when travelling in winter.
1 Snow blocks were set out in a ring and their top surfaces cut to a slope.

2 More blocks of the same size were laid over the first ring, leaning slightly inwards.

3 After three or four rows the dome was completed with one block in the hole in the top.

4 A hole was cut in the wall, or a tunnel dug to the outside.

Below *Igdlus* were more permanent winter houses.
1 The shape of the house and the sleeping platform were cut into the ground.

2 The sleeping platform and the largest roof stones were put in place.

3 The smaller roof stones and the outside walls were built.

4 Turf was laid over the completed house and a seal gut window fitted over the entrance.

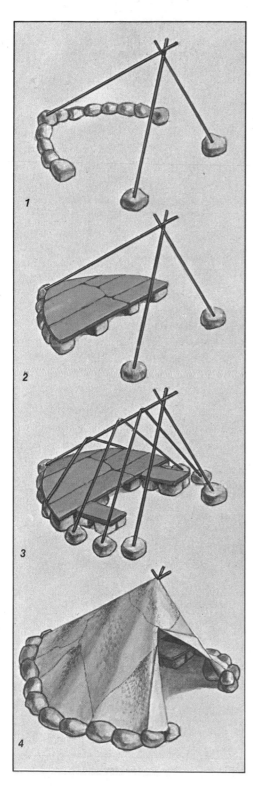

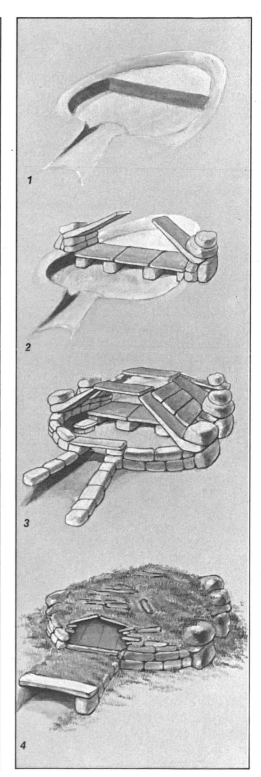

23

At home in an igdlu

The tired dog team hauled the meat-laden sledge round the last headland and picked up speed. Across the bay in the gathering dusk a few spots of yellow light gleamed. Faster and faster the dogs raced along for they knew home and rest were close by.

When the dogs were tied up the Eskimo unloaded the sledge and crawled through the entrance passage into his *igdlu*.

Inside the *igdlu*

Inside, the air was warm and rich with the smell of cooking meat. The flickering light of the blubber lamps lit up the rock walls and the massive stone slabs which formed the low sloping roof of the house.

The Eskimo's wife and her old mother sat in their usual places on the sleeping platform. They wore only their fox-skin pants, for the blubber lamps on which the meat was cooking made the air warm. The meat was walrus which the Eskimo's wife cut from the lump on the stone floor.

A secure base

After he had found space to sit on the sleeping platform the Eskimo carefully placed his clothing to dry on the drying rack which hung over the cooking lamp. When the family had eaten their fill of walrus meat, taken from the stone pot with their fingers, there was still work to be done. The man had to repair his sledging and hunting equipment. His wife had skins to prepare for clothing.

It was a long time before the adults crawled under the caribou skins and joined their children in sleep.

Life in such an *igdlu* was cramped, but simple and well ordered. It was the secure base from which the Eskimo set out on his never-ending hunt for food.

24

In an *igdlu* such as this Polar Eskimo families spent the long Arctic winters. The warmth from the blubber lamps rose and kept the air temperature on the sleeping platform at a comfortable level. In the passage it was quite cold, but close under the roof it was so warm that the Eskimos made a hole which they called "the nose" because of the steam which rose from it.

The family

Life in the Arctic was hard for the Eskimos and the various jobs a family had to do were divided between husband and wife. The woman looked after the skin clothes and prepared the food. The man did the hunting and made and repaired the weapons and tools.

The husband and wife worked as a team. An Eskimo would have thought it very strange not to be married for his wife was very necessary to him.

Small groups

The man and his wife lived with their children and old parents. Eskimos did not often live together in large bands or tribes. It was easier and more sensible to live in small groups as they were continually moving in search of food. If a large number of people stayed in one place, they used up the food supply too quickly.

In the spring or autumn, however, several families joined together to hunt walrus or caribou, or at a fishing camp. At such times the Eskimo families returned to places where there were houses or tent sites which they used every year.

The results of the hunting were shared equally amongst those present. It was a splendid occasion for meeting friends, swapping stories and for young people to form friendships, perhaps leading to marriage.

A new family

The Eskimos had no organized laws and ceremonies as we have come to understand them. Thus there was no formal Eskimo marriage. The new "family" simply lived with either set of parents until they had collected enough skins, and made the necessary tools, to enable them to set up home on their own.

Above Children learn survival skills at an early age. This girl from Victoria Island, Canada has just caught a fine Arctic char.

Left In 1923 Knud Rasmussen met this Netsilik boy called Tertaq. He had 80 amulets which were intended to make him a great hunter.

Below Kagssaluk, a Polar Eskimo woman, and her children, Natu and Inuterk, in their skin tent at Siorapaluk. Sixty-seven years later Inuterk, by then called Inuterssuak, was still living in Siorapaluk (see page 37).

Children

When a crying baby broke the peace of a snow-covered winter house the Eskimos believed it was crying for its name. Choosing a name was a matter of great importance. With it a child received all the skills and qualities of character of the name's previous owner.

Together with a name, a young Eskimo was given a number of amulets, or charms, by the *angakok*, or magician. Among them could have been a hare's foot, so that the child would become a speedy runner like the hare. A raven's beak ensured that the child was always present when animals were killed.

Relaxation

Eskimo children were given great affection and freedom by their parents, and were rarely punished.

Although life was sometimes hard for a child there were times when they could relax. At such times toys like the *ayagak* were produced. (The method of using this is explained on page 44.)

Childhood was the time when the young Eskimos learnt many of the skills which they needed in order to survive when they grew up. Many games trained them in speed and accuracy, which were both very useful to hunters.

Right During their rare moments of leisure the Eskimos enjoyed making toys for their children. Many of the toys were models of things such as sledges which the Eskimos were very familiar with. Others were games which taught the children some of the skills they needed in later life. Such games provided entertainment for the children and for everybody who was watching.

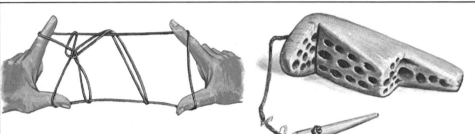

Above Cat's cradle was very popular. This one represents a caribou.

Above An *ayagak;* the piece of bone should be jerked on to the pointer.

Above A decorated leather covered ball from Alaska.

Above A leather ball, and a game made of two smaller balls joined by string.

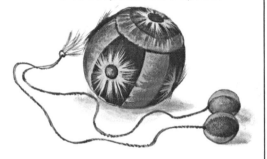

Above Toy ice scoops and a model fish spear.

Above Bows and arrows and a spear with ivory points.

Above a dog team and sledge carved from ivory.

Above Models of ivory snow knives used for cutting snow blocks for igloos

Sila: the Great Spirit

"All true wisdom is to be found far from the dwellings of men, in the great solitudes: and it can only be attained through suffering. Suffering and privation are the only things that can open the mind of man to that which is hidden from his fellows."
Igjugarjuk, a Caribou Eskimo, 1922

The Eskimos thought that there was a great force called *Sila* which controlled everything. They did not think of *Sila* as a person. It was a force which was always present, watching and controlling. The power of *Sila* was universal. At times when hunting was bad, or disease struck the Eskimos, *Sila* was consulted through the *angakok* or magician.

Tupilaks

As well as *Sila* the Eskimos had a number of other spirits which they called *tupilaks*. A *tupilak* was usually an ugly spirit monster created by an Eskimo to carry out a task. This might have been to kill an enemy or just to teach him or her a good lesson!

The unfortunate thing about *tupilaks* was that they were not always reliable. They could always turn on their original owners.

Drums and songs

Tupilaks were one way of settling quarrels. A more open way was the drum dance or song contest. The contest took place near the camp where several families had gathered for the hunting. No one wanted to miss such an occasion which would be talked about for a long time.

Stripped to the waist, the opponents faced each other, and took it in turns to sing and beat their flat, circular drums. The one who was the rudest, or sang the loudest, won.

The following words were sung by a Caribou Eskimo called Piuvkak whose life had been threatened by Qaqortineq after Piuvkak had eaten his store of musk-ox meat:

*"But here I am
to douse you with my mockery,
to deluge you with laughter,
a cheap correction,
easy punishment!"*

Right *Tupilaks* from various parts of the Arctic. In order to create a *tupilak* the Eskimos first carved it in ivory or soft stone. Then its spirit was told what task it had to do. Although you can see that most *tupilaks* were rather ugly, not all of them had bad intentions.

Right The Angmagssalik Eskimos Nujapik and Kuitse at a drumming competition in 1906.

The angakok

"The great sea stirs me, the great sea sets me adrift. It sways me like the weed on a river stone. The sky's height stirs me, the strong wind blows through my mind. It carries me with it, so I shake with joy."

A song which always sent the angakok *Uvavnuk* of the Iglulik Eskimos into a trance

Below Ajuktok, an *angakok* from Angmagssalik in East Greenland, photographed in 1908.

Inside the winter house a half naked figure lay on the fur-covered sleeping platform. The light from several seal-oil lamps shone on his skin and lit up the faces of the men, women and children who sat all around.

Suddenly with a loud shout the figure sat upright and slowly opened his eyes. Quietly he announced that he had just returned from a meeting with *Sedna*, the goddess who lived at the bottom of the sea.

Sedna

It was *Sedna* who sent the animals out into the land and the sea each year. To please her, an Eskimo always put fresh water on the lips of an animal he had killed, so that the animal's spirit was not thirsty.

It was because they were worried about hunting that this small group of Eskimos had gathered in the winter house to consult their *angakok*, as the magician was called.

The *angakok*

The *angakok* always sang a magic song which sent him into a trance. In his trance he went on journeys far across the land, to the bottom of the sea, or even to the sun or the moon.

On this occasion *Sedna* had said that the hunting would be good so everyone was happy.

When a child came home one day and told how he had spoken to a spirit, his parents knew the child would become an *angakok*. His duties as an *angakok* included organizing drum dances and song contests, and consulting the various spirits about the future. For these services he was rewarded with gifts.

It was not always a good thing to be an *angakok*. If he gave bad news, or if his good news was wrong, the group might decide to banish him.

30

Below An amulet belt collected by Knud Rasmussen in 1924. On it are owl's claws, to give strong fists: wolf bones to give strong legs: and the head of a great Northern diver, to make the wearer a good hunter.

Bottom A Thule chain of the sort made by the Polar Eskimos of the Thule region of North Greenland. Each small carving represents a different part of their "chain of life". Amongst them are a man and a woman, a sledge, a *kayak,* an igloo, a seal, a raven, a walrus and in the centre the head of *Nanok,* the bear.

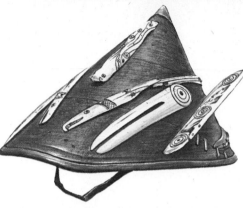

Left A hunting hat from Alaska, made of wood and decorated with ivory charms.

Below Carved wooden dance mask from Diomede Island, Bering Straits.

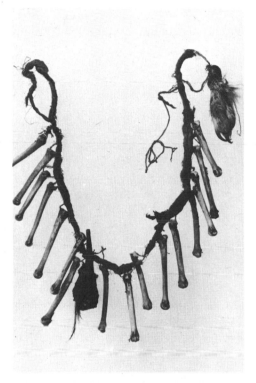

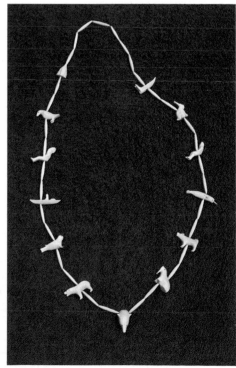

The Eskimos loved to listen to a good story in the long hours of winter darkness. Since they had no written language, stories were the only way traditions and history could be passed from one generation to another. The storytellers were either the *angakoks* or the old folks. In the flickering light of the blubber lamps they could hold a large audience spellbound.

Above An *aussik* was an imaginary animal like a snake or a worm. It lived in the mountains and occasionally came out to chase the Eskimos.

Border A selection of walrus tusks decorated with scrimshaw. Some have been made into pipes and one into a counting board for a game called cribbage. All of the tusks were made in the Alaskan Arctic in the late 19th century. The Eskimos learned scrimshaw decoration from the many whalers who visited the area at that time.

How Sedna Rules in the Sea

Sedna was once a pretty young orphan girl. One day her guardian tried to drown her because he did not want to look after her any longer. But she clung to the side of his boat and he had to cut off her fingers before she would sink to the bottom of the sea. Since then she has lived on the sea bed. Her hair has become long and tangled because without fingers she cannot hold a comb.

When she appeared among them the sea creatures began to take refuge in her hair whenever the Eskimos broke one of their rules. If that happened an *angakok* had to be sent down to comb *Sedna's* hair out. Not until he had done this and made *Sedna* happy again were the creatures freed, and not until they were freed could the Eskimos hunt them again.

The Song of the Lemming

On a cold winter's day a little lemming came out of his warm hole. He looked about him, shivered, shook himself, and sang:
"The sky,
like a vast belly,
arches itself around my burrow.
The air is clear,
no cloud in sight :
icy weather ! Aiee !
I'm freezing ! freezing !"

The Bear Who Fell in Love

A young bear once fell in love with a little Eskimo woman. Every day, when the woman's husband was out hunting for the bear, he would creep into the woman's igloo.

While they were together one day the bear said to the woman, "Little woman, I live high up in the mountains, you go this way, and that way, and this way again. My igloo is very beautiful but I should like a wife to share it – a wife like you!"

Then the bear added, "But don't ever tell your husband who is hunting me where I live; remember if you do I shall hear it in my heart."

Many days and weeks passed and the woman's husband had still not caught the bear and he was very unhappy. One night the woman could not keep her secret any longer and she cuddled up and whispered to him *"Nanok!"* (bear). "Where?" cried her husband. Very quietly she whispered in his ear, "High up in the mountains, you go this way, and that way, and this way again."

The man set off immediately but when he got there the bear's den was empty. While her husband was gone the frightened woman lay on the sleeping platform until she heard a sort of thunder rolling down the mountains. It was he, the great bear, can you hear him?

He ran, he breathed, he went straight to the igloo, he was going to crush it! He raised an enormous paw. No, he only swept the roof and passed. His back bent, his legs gave way, his arms hung like those of a tired old bear.

Betrayed and unhappy, he set off across the ice with two big tears running down his shiny black nose.

The Raven and the Goose

Do you know why the raven is so black, so dull and black in colour? It is all because of its own obstinacy. Now listen.

It all happened in the days when all birds were getting their colours and the pattern in their coats. And the raven and the goose happened to meet, and they agreed to paint each other. The raven began and painted the other black with a nice white pattern showing between.

The goose thought that very fine indeed, and began to do the same to the raven, painting it a coat exactly like its own.

But the raven fell into a rage, and declared that the pattern was frightfully ugly, and the goose, offended at all the fuss, simply splashed it black all over. And now you know why the raven is black.

Qadlunat

*"An island of wood appeared alongside the ice.
It moved across the sea with wings.
It had many houses and rooms deep
in its belly with many noisy people."*
**Nauja, a Cape York Eskimo woman, describing the
arrival of John Ross's ship in 1818**

Below Captain John Ross meeting the Polar Eskimos in 1818. The painting was done by Captain Ross's Eskimo interpreter, Hans Zakaeus. He put himself in the right of the picture wearing a top hat.

In the picture at the bottom of the page are Dr. John Rae and a group of Eskimos at Pelly Bay. The Eskimos showed him items from the Franklin expedition and were able to tell him where the explorers had died. As a result Rae received part of the reward which had been offered for discovering the fate of Franklin.

Captain John Ross was probably as surprised as the Thule Eskimos of Cape York when in 1818 he met a party of them travelling over the ice.

Ross was the leader of a British naval expedition searching for a north-west passage to India and the east. He was the first non-Eskimo the Eskimos living in northern Greenland had ever seen. When Ross said that he came from the south the Eskimos were amazed. "How can that be?" they said, "That is where all our ice goes to in summer".

The north-west passage
The desire to find a north-west passage to India reached a peak in the mid-19th century. Many expeditions set sail from Europe on the dangerous and lengthy voyage up into the Arctic. Suddenly the Eskimo's lands were being invaded by these strange *qadlunat* (white men) from the south.

Right In the year A.D.982 a Viking called Erik the Red sailed from Iceland to Greenland. In the following years the Norsemen, or Vikings, established two settlements in South Greenland. After about 300 years the settlement died out and nobody knows why.

There are some stories which suggest that the Norsemen attacked the Eskimos but were finally driven out by them. This woodcut by Aron, an Eskimo from Kangeq, shows Norsemen attacking an Eskimo camp.

After the Franklin tragedy, when in 1847 a whole expedition starved to death in the Arctic, a new type of explorer appeared. Men like Leopold McClintock and John Rae did not rely on heavy equipment packed in London, as the explorers before them had done. They travelled light, made friends with the Eskimos, and learned from them the way to survive.

The whalers

The whalers followed such explorers, who had told of the rich whaling grounds of Baffin Bay and the Beaufort Sea. Their only aim was to make money and they plundered the Arctic seas and its peoples. They pursued the great whales for oil and baleen. The oil was sold for a high price in Europe. The baleen, which was a flexible material found in the mouths of whales, was much in demand for ladies' corset stays.

The whalers penetrated deep into the Arctic and they introduced the Eskimos to such things as iron and rifles. Such items made the Eskimos' life much easier. But the other things the whalers brought, such as tobacco, alcohol and disease, had a bad effect.

By the end of the 19th century the whaling grounds were exhausted. The whaling fleets vanished from the Arctic seas, but the Eskimo's way of life had changed forever.

An Eskimo visits the *qadlunat*

In 1728 an Eskimo in a *kayak* paddled up the River Don in Aberdeen. He was dressed in sealskins and very tired. After a few days he caught a cold and died. Nobody knows how he came to be there. Perhaps he had been caught in the pack ice. You can see the lonely Eskimo's *kayak* in the museum in Aberdeen.

Left This drawing from William Scoresby's *Account of the Arctic Regions* shows how dangerous whaling could be.

Below Tulluachiu and his family were great friends of John Ross. Their friendship was encouraged by the fine wooden leg which the ship's carpenter made for him. The leg had an inscription on it which read, "*Victory, June 1831*".

35

"When the devil was asleep...."

"The Devil is asleep or having trouble with his wife, or we should never have come back so easily."
Ootah, who accompanied Peary to the North Pole in 1909, on their return to land

At the end of the 19th century explorers turned their attention from the north-west passage to the problems of more general exploration. Most of them adopted the Eskimos' methods of travel and survival. Foremost amongst these was Commander Robert Peary of the US Navy. Together with four Polar Eskimos, including Ootah, Peary reached the North Pole, or "big nail" as the Eskimos called it, in 1909.

Jørgen Brønlund

Brønlund was an Eskimo who accompanied a Danish expedition to North East Greenland in 1906. Brønlund set out with two others on a sledge journey from which none of them returned. The following spring a search party found his body. His diary told what had happened:

"Perished in 79 fjord after trying to return across the Inland ice. I came here in a waning moon and could not get any further because of my frost-bitten feet. The bodies of the others can be found in the middle of the fjord in front of the glacier".

Brønlund knew how important his party's diaries and maps were. He had struggled on to a place where he knew they would be found.

Knud Rasmussen

Rasmussen was known to his Eskimo friends as "the one whose laugh goes before him". He founded a trading post at Thule in North Greenland which he used as a base for his Thule expeditions. His greatest journey was the Fifth Thule Expedition. Over a period of four years he dog-sledged a total of 35,000km from North Greenland, across Canada to the Pacific. By the 1920s, his traditional Eskimo methods were being replaced by modern techniques.

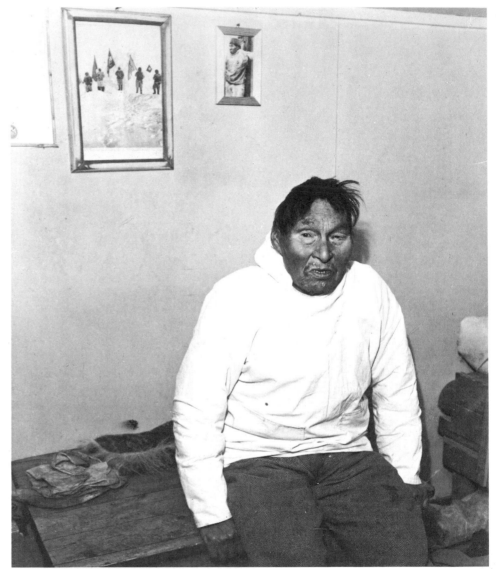

Above The Polar Eskimo Ootah who accompanied Commander Peary's party to the North Pole. Ootah is seen here in his house at Qanaq. On the wall is a copy of Peary's photograph of the group at the North Pole. After the expedition Ootah was made a member of the Explorers' Club of New York.

Left Jørgen Brønlund and his fellow Eskimo Tobias Gabrielsen assembling a sledge before the start of their fateful journey.

Left As a young man Inuterssuak Uvdloriak travelled widely across the Arctic with a number of British and Danish expeditions.

In 1978 he was still living in Siorapaluk where he was the leader of the village council. He is seen as a child on page 26.

Right On most of his expeditions Inuterssuak was accompanied by his wife Naduk. She looked after the expedition's fur clothing.

Below Harald Moltke painted this picture of Knud Rasmussen after an expedition together.

After Thule

Below Copper Eskimos trading white fox furs at Cape Dufferin, Hudson Bay, Canada.

When the whalers left the Arctic at the end of the 19th century, more white men arrived. Fur traders began to move into the Canadian Arctic. They persuaded many Eskimos to give up their traditional hunting, and to trap fur-bearing animals instead. The animals were not trapped for their meat but because trading companies wanted their fur to sell. The Eskimos were paid in guns, ammunition, tobacco and tinned food.

The white man's civilization

At first the Eskimos welcomed the products of the white man's civilization. The weapons gave them a new mastery of the animals. But they had no such mastery of the white man and became increasingly dependent on their trade with him.

The traders were followed by missionaries and government officials. These new invaders were determined to convert the Eskimos to what they considered a better and more civilized way of life. The Eskimos were encouraged to live in permanent settlements close to the trading posts and missionaries. But the white man's schooling and religion did not fit the Eskimos for a life of hunting, or for life in the "civilized" world.

A confused people

Because so many people were living close together in settlements, hunting became more difficult. As a result the Eskimos became even more dependent on the white man. Alcohol, tobacco, vice and disease did further harm to people who were already confused.

The *angakoks* were powerless to help their people. The Thule way of life, which had dominated the Arctic for a thousand years, was ended.

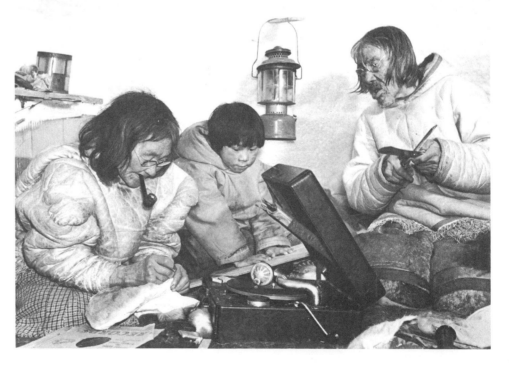

38

Above Once the Eskimos obtained modern rifles their methods of seal hunting changed. Instead of the crawling and waiting necessary to hunt by the *utok* method, the Eskimos could shoot their seals from many yards away. They still needed to approach unseen and to do this they used a screen of white fabric. The rifle fitted through a hole in the middle of the screen so the Eskimo could shoot while hiding behind the screen.

Left Caribou Eskimos listening to a gramophone in their igloo at Baker Lake, Northwest Territories, Canada.

Right The Greenland Eskimos obtained glass beads in trade from the whalers. At first the beads were used to decorate their traditional clothing. But since the mid-19th century their national costume has been developed using much beadwork.

kikutdlūnît pôrskime
tugsiakátârusugtut
sungiusariarsiñáuput
arfiningornerme únúkut
nal. 19 atuarfingmut.

Above Sign written in Greenland Eskimo, inviting the Eskimos to an Easter service in the local church.

Above Canadian Eskimo "syllabics". The Eskimo language was not written down until the white man came to the Arctic.

The present

"You made a picture of us in your minds, you whites, now you believe the picture.
You do not even know our name. You call us Eskimo. That is an Indian word. We are Inuit, we are the people of this land!"
Jonasee, an Eskimo from Frobisher Bay

In the towns which have grown in the Arctic in the past 20-30 years many of the Eskimos live in neat government houses, and some of them work for various trading companies or government departments. Their children go to government schools and wear clothes bought from the store.

Hospitals, shops and cars make their life easier. Helicopters and aircraft buzz through the air like the familiar midges in summer. Everywhere (except in Greenland) motor sledges replace dog teams.

Regrets
Some Eskimos enjoy the new life but many are confused by the "advantages" of the white man's civilization. They live in towns or settlements but are unable to adjust to such a life. In their hearts they wish to live as the old Eskimos. They regret that in the government schools their children are learning only the white man's ways and the Eskimo values of self respect and self reliance are being forgotten.

Such people feel they have lost their identity. They cannot go hunting because the animals avoid the settlements. In many cases there is no white man's work for them, but the Eskimos resent having to take the white man's "welfare" payments.

The white man's road
Because of these problems Canadian Eskimos who do not wish to follow the white man's road have formed *Inuit* associations. They are trying to persuade the government that the Arctic land, its animals and raw materials, belong to the Eskimos.

If they succeed they will have some control of their future and the Eskimo way of life will not be lost.

Above In many areas of Canada it was the early traders of the Hudson Bay Company who made the first contacts with the Eskimos. Now the trading posts are big modern stores. They trade in a great variety of goods, including the skidoos seen here. Skidoos have replaced almost all the dog teams in Canada and Alaska.

Left Packing shrimps for export is a well established industry in Greenland. These Eskimo women are working in a small factory at Upernavik.

Above The midnight sun over Kungmiut, East Greenland. The policy of the Danish government has been to control outside influence in Greenland. They have allowed some small hunting communities such as this to remain. As a result the Greenland Eskimos lead a more traditional life than their Canadian brothers.

Right This house has most modern facilities, but the floor is the only place to cut up a seal.

Below In many towns and settlements much of the housing is of low standard.

The way ahead

"Our way of life will change, but let us do it in our time, in our own way."

A spokesman for Inuit Tapirisat, *addressing Prime Minister Trudeau of Canada*

With the rapid expansion of the oil and mining industries there are many changes taking place in the Arctic. In Canada an organization called *Inuit Tapirisat*, the Eskimo Brotherhood, is trying to limit these changes where they will be bad for the Eskimos. In Greenland there is a similar organization called *Siumut*.

Greenland

Greenland, which is part of Denmark, is governed by a parliament which is run by the Eskimos themselves. They also face some of the same problems as the Eskimos in Canada and Alaska. But because of careful control of developments which affect them, the Greenland Eskimos have been more fortunate. Many of them, especially the Polar Eskimos, have continued to live a traditional hunting life.

The new *angakoks*

In Canada and Greenland the Eskimos who still go out hunting and living on the land are highly respected. But even out in the spaces of the Arctic things have changed.

Where the Eskimos once roamed unhindered new *angakoks* are at work: the white men busy extracting oil, gas and minerals.

In Greenland and the north American Arctic a number of coal, lead and zinc mines are operating. Out among the islands of the Beaufort Sea and along the west coast of Greenland, geologists have found large oil and gas deposits under the sea. Such deposits are the basis of a rapidly expanding new industry.

Throughout the Arctic there is much similiar activity. Great construction projects and hydro-electric schemes are under way. Across the tundra, trucks leave deep

Above An above-ground section of the Alaska pipeline. Naturalists are very concerned about the effects such pipelines have on the ground and on animals near them.

Left Schools throughout the Arctic are helping to educate young Eskimos so that they better understand the new developments which are taking place.

Below Now they cannot live off hunting the Eskimos must learn new skills. These boys are at a typing class in Churchill, Manitoba, Canada.

tracks which will last for centuries. Pipelines weave across the Arctic landscape, obstructing the migration of the remaining caribou.

Such schemes create pollution. All of them threaten to change the Eskimos' land by disturbing the plant and animal life. The feelings of the Eskimos are summed up by Elijah Takkiapik of the Fort Chimo community council:

"We very much dislike white people taking our land for granted. It seems that they feel that they can destroy our land any time they feel like it without even asking for permission. They steal the raw materials without even consulting us or giving the *Inuit* a percentage of what they are taking. We need to get power to control the land."

Power over the land

For thousands of years the Eskimos had a sense of identity as a group, and a deep understanding of their own way of life. Modern developments have overtaken this understanding and left the Eskimos as onlookers in their own land. It is the control of the land which mainly concerns *Inuit Tapirisat*. They are negotiating with the government to obtain control of it for the Eskimos.

Education will be important. Eskimos are now taking charge of their own schools. Their children will learn about the wider world. But they will also learn the Eskimo way of life and will have the chance to live it on a land which is truly theirs.

Through *Inuit Tapirisat* and *Siumut* the Eskimo voice is at last being heard. If the world listens the Eskimos will be able to regain their self respect and sense of identity. And the Arctic will once again become *Inuit Nunangat*: The People's Land.

Above One successful industry which is entirely Eskimo is the production of carvings and prints. An Eskimo co-operative collects the work and markets it all over the world.

Left In Greenland each small community has its council which reports the community's views to the Greenland parliament. This is a council meeting at Qanaq, the home of the Polar Eskimos.

Things to do

Making an *ayagak*

1. Obtain a 100mm (4″) long, 40mm (1½″) diameter piece of bone from a butcher. When it is clean, drill a large hole in the end and a small hole through the centre. Tie the bone to a 150mm (6″) piece of tapered wood with a 350mm (14″) length of string. A simpler and easier version can be made with a tube of rolled card tied to a pencil.

2. To play the game, hold the pencil with the roll hanging down. Flick the roll up and try to catch it with the pencil through the hole in the end. It's harder than it looks!

A model igloo

Eskimos build igloos by cutting blocks of snow from the ground and spiralling them upwards into a dome. Build a model igloo the same way, but using dough instead of snow. You will need a knife, a 180mm (7″) plate, a pencil, a baseboard and white icing. (A real igloo would use fewer blocks, see P.23.)

1. Draw a circle on the baseboard round the plate. Roll out the dough into a 10mm (½″) thick slab big enough to cut out about 50 blocks roughly 40mm (1½″) long by 25mm (1″) wide.

2. Lay four blocks in line and cut them diagonally as shown. Trim the sides so that they fit round the circle. Glue them down with icing.

3. Continue trimming blocks and glueing them down to complete the circle. When you reach the sloped blocks, trim the bottoms as well as the sides so that the next layer tilts inwards a little.

4. Continue spiralling upwards tilting each layer a little more until you reach the top of the dome. Fill the centre hole with a block cut to fit.

5. Cut a doorway two blocks high and build a porch as an arch of smaller blocks. Paint the igloo and base with icing "snow": add Eskimo and sledge.

A model *kayak*

Make a model *kayak* the way Eskimos make them. We will use glue instead of leather thongs to join the framework. You will need : thin card or thick paper, scissors, balsa cement, tweezers and Cling-Wrap, Fablon or sticky tape to cover the framework.

1. Cut the profile shape (top right) 293mm (9″) long from the card.

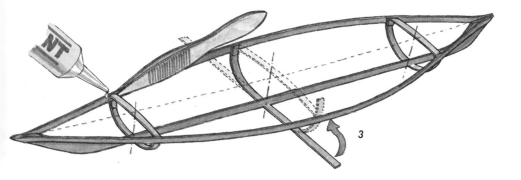

2. Cut two strips of card 3mm ($\frac{1}{8}$″) wide and 260mm (10″) long and glue them, one each side from front to back to form the deck-line.

3. Cut more strips and glue in three ribs. Glue them square to the bottom and when dry, curve them up to join the deck strips. Add deck frames to curve the ribs and deckline strips correctly.

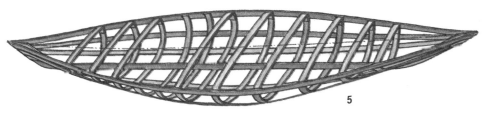

4. Cut four more long strips and glue two more each side from front to rear between deck-line strips and bottom. Glue wherever they touch a rib, and at front and back. Trim off excess to fit *kayak* shape.

5. Add more ribs, glueing wherever they touch the long strips. Add more deck-frames, tailoring them to fit. Leave a gap for the cockpit coaming. It helps always to work from one side to the other.

6. Make the cockpit coaming shown below with cross strips to support it in the boat's framework.

Coaming

7. Glue the coaming into position and fix deck side frames. Cut six more strips, tapered at the ends and glue them on the deck wherever they cross deck frames.

8. The finished frame is surprisingly strong and ready for covering with film or tape. Use small pieces to avoid wrinkles. Paint with matt grey or fawn plastic model enamel and add Eskimo and paddle, cut from card and painted as shown.

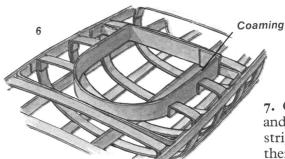

Reference

The year of the Eskimo	
Sekiliniak "*the sun appears*"	January
Arkajuassuak "*it is warm*"	April
Agpaliarssuit tikitarfiat "*the birds return*"	May
Tingmissat erniviat "*they have eggs*"	June
Ivnanit aorsarnialertarfiat "*new born birds fly south*"	August
Talsit sikoutat "*the lakes freeze*"	September
Tousarfit "*one listens*"	November

Language

The Eskimo language is spoken by all the tribes throughout the Arctic, with local dialects in some areas. It is very complicated: often one long word replaces what would be a whole sentence in English.

Tugto means "a caribou".
Tugtossuak means "a big caribou".
Tugtossuaksiok means "hunt a big caribou".
Tugtossuaksiokniak means "will hunt a big caribou".
Tugtossuaksiokniakpunga means "I will hunt a big caribou".

Here are more Eskimo words:

Nanok : bear	*Puise* : seal
Kringmek : dog	*Amarok* : wolf
Auvek : walrus	*Teriangniak* : fox
Mana : now	*Uvdlume* : today
Igdlu : house	*Nuna* : land
Siko : ice	*Kamutit* : sledge
Anori : wind	*Aput* : snow
Okorto : warm	*Ise* : cold
Ariarnatok : good	*Ajorpok* : bad

Eskimo numerals

1 *Atasuk*
2 *Makluk*
3 *Pingasuk*
4 *Sisamut*
5 *Tavdlumat*
6 *Arfinek*
7 *Arfinek Makluk*
8 *Arfinek Pingasuk*
9 *Kulaikluat*
10 *Kulit*

Books

Interesting books for younger readers are *Modern Eskimos*, by Mary Bringle, Franklin Watts, *Alaska and its Wild Life*, by Sage, Hamlyn, and *A Closer Look at Eskimos*, Hamish Hamilton. *Eskimos* by Wally Herbert, Collins, is an illustrated account for older readers. *The book of the Eskimo* by Peter Freuchen, Fawcett World Library, is by a Dane who lived with the Eskimos for many years. *The People of the Deer* by Farley Mowat, Seven Seas Publishing Company, is a tragic account of the last days of a group of Caribou Eskimos. One collection of poems, translated from Danish, is *Eskimo Poems from Canada and Greenland*, Allison and Busby.

Scrub Dog of Alaska by Walt Morey, Sidgwick and Jackson, is about a pup's struggle to survive after being thrown out by Smiley Jackson, who breeds dog teams.

Julie of the Wolves by Jean Craighead George, Puffin, is the story of Julie, or Miyax, who becomes lost in the Arctic.

Miki by Palle Petersen, Franklin Watts, is about a Greenland puppy who joins a dog team.

The Blind Boy and the Loon by Ramona Maher, Aberlard Schuman, is a book of traditional stories, illustrated with modern Eskimo art.

Sources of Information

Good sources are *Inuit Tapirisat* of Canada, 176 Gloucester Street, Ottawa, Canada; the Canadian High Commission, Canada House, Trafalgar Square, London SW1; the Danish Embassy, 55 Sloane Street, London SW1; *Atuagagdliutit*, the Greenland Eskimo newspaper, PO Box 39, Godthab, 3900 Greenland.

Museums

The Museum of Mankind, London
The Horniman Museum, London
The City Museum, Liverpool
The University Museum of Archaeology, Cambridge
The Danish National Museum, Copenhagen
The Museum of Man, Ottawa
The city museums of some old whaling ports like Hull have collections.

Above The Eskimos did not divide the year into weeks and months as we do. Their year was controlled by the world of nature around them. They recognized seven seasons, and gave them names to suit the different yearly events which happened in them.

One listened in November because the ice had formed and travelling was possible. Groups were able to meet and many stories were exchanged.

The Eskimo calendar makes a good subject for collage pictures, using simple materials: blue and white felt for September, for example.

What can we learn?

We have many things such as railways, TV and big cities, which many Eskimos have never seen. But as well as these advantages we have wars and crime. We pollute our seas and rivers. Side by side with wealth we have great poverty.

Some of these problems we have passed on to the Eskimos: in their old way of life they knew none of them.

Eskimos made their living from the natural things around them. Because of this they caused no pollution, and their methods of hunting did not threaten to kill all of the animals.

Above all the Eskimos were a happy people: their needs were simple and they did not worry about what would happen tomorrow. If an Eskimo owned one good sledge and dog team he would be admired, but if he had two his friends laughed at him.

They always shared their food. Their children grew up close to their parents, watching them until they were able to be independent.

A long time ago the Eskimos thought they were the only people on the earth and called themselves *inuit*: the people or the men. Their way of life required courage: it also required patience, fellow feeling and understanding. Can we claim to have these virtues too?

Glossary

Amulets were pieces of animals or birds, such as bones or beaks, which were given to young children. They were supposed to give the children the qualities of the animals from which the amulets came.

Baleen The name of the long plates in the mouth of a whale which filter out plankton from the sea. It was because the baleen was much in demand for such things as corset stays and hat bands that so many whalers went to the Arctic.

Coaming Raised border on *kayaks* to prevent sea water coming in.

Culture The way of life developed by a particular group of people at a certain time. Thus the Dorset Culture was the way of life of the Dorset Eskimos. After 3000 years they disappeared and the Thule Culture became the most important.

Eskimo Algonquin Indian word (*uskimawak*) for "one who eats raw meat". It was adopted as *Esquimaux* by the French, and passed into English as Eskimo.

Igdlu The Eskimo word for any sort of house constructed of snow, rock, turf or timber.

Igloo The white man's version of *igdlu*, used for a snow house only.

Insulator Something which separates. Each part of an Eskimo's clothing had to be a good insulator to help separate his warm body from the extreme cold outside.

Kooletah The caribou fur coat which the Polar Eskimos use.

Lichen Small, slow growing plants, a mixture of fungus and algae.

Migration Moving with the seasons. Some animals, such as the caribou, and most birds, migrate from the Arctic in autumn so that they can spend the Arctic winter somewhere warmer. They return in spring.

Narwhal A small whale about 5m long, with a spiral tusk up to 3m long.

Plankton Small creatures, just one cell in size, which live in the sea. They rise to the surface in spring and multiply due to the increased sunlight.

Sinew The fibrous material which connects bones and muscles in animals.

Important dates

15,000-10,000BC The first Eskimos began to spread into the Arctic from Asia.

3,000-2,500BC Eskimos reached the northern tip of Greenland.

AD1576 The first known contact between Eskimos and white men. Martin Frobisher sailing from England discovered the eastern Canadian Arctic. He captured some Eskimos and as a result they took some of his crew prisoner.

1724 Two Eskimos, Poek and Qiperoq, were sent from Greenland to Copenhagen by Hans Egede the Greenland Bishop. They took part in *kayak* races on the canals and upset the Danish king by harpooning the ducks on his palace pond.

1789 Alexander Mackenzie crossed the tundra to the river that now bears his name and made contact with the Mackenzie Eskimos.

1818 Captain John Ross of the Royal Navy sailed into Baffin Bay and became the first white man to meet the Polar Eskimos.

1820 Captain Clavering in charge of HMS *Griper* discovered a small group of Eskimos living in north east Greenland.

1830 The first Hudson Bay Company trading post established at Fort Chimo in the Canadian arctic.

1862-68 Kridlarssuak, chief of the Baffin Island Eskimos led an expedition of his people to visit the Polar Eskimos of Greenland.

1884 Lt. Gustav Holm of the Danish Navy led an expedition which discovered the previously unknown East Greenland Eskimos.

1908-12 Vilhjalmur Stefansson explored the Canadian Arctic from Alaska to Coronation Gulf, and discovered the Copper Eskimos.

April 6, 1909 Commander Robert Peary and Mathew Henson, together with Polar Eskimos Ootah, Ooqueah, Seegloo and Egingwah became the first people to reach the North Pole.

1921-24 Knud Rasmussen made his 5th Thule Expedition from Greenland to Hudson Bay, and from there by dog sledge through the Canadian Arctic to Siberia. He met all the Eskimo tribes and found they all spoke the same language.

1947-54 More than 300 Eskimos starved to death in the Keewatin province of Canada, due to decreasing numbers of caribou. At this time the Eskimo population of Canada had dropped to 8000. (There are now 22,000 Eskimos in Canada.)

1971 The organisation *Inuit Tapirisat* of Canada was formed. Its main purpose was to establish the Eskimo's claim to ownership of the Arctic lands.

1976 *Inuit Tapirisat* offered the Canadian Government a gift of over a million square kilometres of the Eskimos' land. The remaining land was to be Eskimo property and called *Nunavut*, Our Land.

Acknowledgements

The publishers wish to acknowledge the help of Mr Barry Dufour in the initial stages of the planning of this book.

Photographs
Key: T top; B bottom; L left; R right; C centre.

Bryan & Cherry Alexander: 2-3, 11(BR), 18-19, 39(T), 40(T), cover.
Ardea: 26(T).
Arktisk Institut, Denmark 29(R), 36(B).
Bo Bojesen: 40(B), 43(B).
British Petroleum: 42(T).
Fred Bruemmer: 42(BL).
Canada Phototheque/Terry Pearce: 42(BR).
Van Cleve Photography: 28.
Bruce Coleman: 8(T), 8(B), 10(TL), 10-11.
Daily Telegraph/Peter Juul: 41(BR), 43(T).
Mary Evans Picture Library: 35(B).
Derek Fordham: 14-15, 22, 31(L), 37(TL), 37(TR), 41(T).
Robert Harding Associates: 39(B).
Brian Hawkes: 9, 10(TR), 11(TL), 11(TR).
Horniman Museum/Daisy Hayes: 16-17, 31(R).
Hudson's Bay Company: 34(B).
Alan Hutchison: 41(BL).
National Film Board of Canada: 38(B).
The National Museum of Denmark: 26(BL), 26(BR), 30, 31(T), 35(T), 37(B).
Popperfoto: 38(T).
Radio Times Hulton Picture Library: 34(T).
US Navy: 36(T).